As a Spiritual Psychologist worked in sessions with a significant number of people going through a difficult grieving process, and these are not fun. Unbeknownst to many, the process of grieving does not have to be difficult nor lengthly. It is a part of the human experience and a healthy, as well as natural, consequence of losing something of value. The good news, which Mike has captured so beautifully, is that there are ways that are not that difficult of shifting one's orientation into a more natural process, the result of which is that grieving is healthy as well as finite. I thank Mike for writing this brave book.

> — Ron Hulnick, Pres., University of Santa Monica
> and co-author with Mary R. Hulnick of
> *Loyalty to Your Soul: The Heart of Spiritual Psychology*

In *Healing Through Grief*, Mike Polek weaves an intimate story of his own growth through understanding and embracing grief. His book is also an informational text on how grief affects our bodies, minds, and emotions. He shares stories of his own experiences as well as others, and lays out for us a blueprint of how our beliefs and expectations shape our feelings. He also includes a rare look at the unconscious, which affects our daily lives, most of the time without our knowing. The book leaves us with a powerful exploration of how our choices about how we view loss play an important role in our relationships, especially within our own levels of consciousness.

> — Carol Jones, author of *Through Kenny's Eyes,*
> *A Magnificent Journey from Illness to Ecstasy.*

This book offers practical wisdom and a framework that makes grief make sense. Through understanding *the gap* and how it relates to the stages of grief, readers can examine their perspectives and ultimately come to acceptance and compassion for themselves. The author draws on his personal experience and the field of Spiritual Psychology to create this powerful and inspiring guide to grief. While grieving is a process that can take time and energy move through, this book will make it easier.

— Carrie Doubts, grief and transition coach, founder of Life's Next Chapter Coaching

I was excited to read Mike's book for a few reasons. I had heard about his successful Healing Through Grief workshops that I had not yet been able to attend in person. I have always felt a little awkward around grieving - with my own grief, as well as being with someone else that was experiencing a loss. And the third reason is that I'm an author. And while my story is fiction (an over-the-top action adventure novel) I really wanted my characters to deal with loss and grieving in a real way. I have had a challenge with other stories where the main characters go through traumatic situations and then they're like, "OK, we did it. Let's go get a cheeseburger and celebrate!" Healing through Grief, assisted me both personally and professionally. Thank you, Mike, for writing a caring, insightful, and clear book about a subject that isn't always talked about. My heart is more open to myself and others, and my life is better for reading your book.

— John J. Hruby, author of
Space Spiders on Prom Day

HEALING THROUGH GRIEF

FINDING FREEDOM FROM DEPRESSION

For contact information: www.michaelpolek.com

Cover Art: Michael Polek
Cover: Michael Polek
Book Designer: Michael Polek

Please note that individuals referenced in this work are not specific persons, unless stated as such. The stories that I relate are based upon essential conversations in my work with individuals and groups, with any identifying characteristics (names, etc.) changed. The stories are intended to be instructive illustrations.

ISBN 13: 978-1-7327176-7-1

10 9 8 7 6 5 4 3 2 1

HEALING THROUGH GRIEF

FINDING FREEDOM FROM DEPRESSION

Rev. Michael Polek, M.A., M.S.

Los Angeles, CA, U.S.A.

DEDICATED TO MY PARENTS

Acknowledgements

John-Roger for guidance, both inner and outer.

John Morton for steadfast support.

Derrick Jackson for encouragement and editing.

My parents for their support throughout my life.

My family for being there over the years.

Ron and Mary Hulnick for encouragement and support on many levels. You inspire me.

Michael Hayes and Alisha Das Hayes for sharing their gifts and wisdom.

Christina Suter for forever friendship.

Paula Majeski for all the Moments.

Carol Jones for leadership and loving.

Steve Chandler for words of encouragement.

Licia Rester-Frazee for inspiration and dedication.

John Hruby for guidance and demonstration.

All participants in my workshops for their courage and inspiration.

Face to face with finality
Soul moment
Timeless stillness

To touch stone, cold
Yet afraid
To be burned by ash

Ash and stone awaken in me
The void
Now filled with grief

– Michael Polek

Table of Contents

PREFACE

You are reading my love, made manifest in words. This manuscript is based on my personal experience, the experiences of close friends, and participants in my workshops. I have developed a way of working with the process of grieving that assists people with having a deeper understanding of the complex emotional world of grief and sadness related to a loss. I am offering a potential way out of the cycle of depression that many have used successfully. The way out is not to avoid grieving or postpone it, but rather to use the process of grieving as a healing agent. In this book you will learn how to address the root cause of grief and love your way through it. If these words resonate with you, then this book was written for you.

INTRODUCTION

Please be aware that depression may have diverse causes as well as contributing factors. The ideas expressed in this book may assist you in working through the mental and emotional material associated with depression. Many people that I have worked with one-on-one and in grieving workshops have found these ideas invaluable in their own healing process. For some people, the material they are working with may be beyond the scope of what is offered in these pages. A medical approach may be the most appropriate intervention. Ultimately you, dear reader, are the author of your life. You will decide whether you can benefit from these chapters, or if you must seek elsewhere. If you feel you need professional help in the form of a psychologist or psychiatrist, I encourage you to seek out a mental healthcare professional who can work with you and provide support.

If you are seeking a unique, empowering, compassionate, loving way to work with grief and depression, or perhaps a friend or relative has recommended this book to you, then read on. If even one person picks up this book, reads it, and finds themselves freer, happier, and more in harmony with life than before reading it, then I have fulfilled my purpose in writing it. If you are such a person, I encourage you to write to me and tell me your story, and please let me know if you're willing to have me share it with others. I very much believe that we can all learn from one another and inspire one another through our stories and our experiences.

We are all co-travelers in life. I invite you to journey with me for a little while, exploring new territory, along the path of discovery. May you find freedom.

Chapter 1

Everybody Grieves

In our culture, we don't often talk about death, dying, and grieving until we are faced with it. We are left to figure it out for ourselves. There is no Grief 101 class in high school to assist those who are in the process of grieving, or to help those who have yet to experience a deep sense of loss understand what lies ahead. And yet the grieving process is an experience common to all souls who walk the Earth.

Grief is personal. It can be isolating. It is strange, in a way, that something that everyone experiences is not something that is normally considered a shared experience. Everyone grieves in their own way and in their own timing. To say, "I've been there," while attempting to be supportive, can feel like an intrusion. While I cannot pretend to truly understand your grief, or expect that you will understand mine, I will nevertheless attempt to make a connection by sharing my experience and insight as best as I am able.

In the chapters ahead, I will relate my own experience which forms the basis of my understanding of the grieving process. I will lay out a framework for understanding the process and experience of grieving. I will provide illustrative stories to assist you in anchoring your understanding as well as exercises and questions for exploration to assist you in working with the material in this book as it relates to your own experience with grief and depression. My intention is that everyone reading this book benefit from the information and practical exercises.

While I cannot take away the pain that comes with loss, my hope is that through gaining a greater understanding of grief and depression, how they are related, and how to use the methods presented in this book, you will be better prepared to bring the grieving process to resolution. To illustrate, I begin with my own story.

Chapter 2

My Own Journey

The seeds of this work started with my experiences at the turn of the millennium. Prior to that time, I had had brief bouts of grief from the loss of loved ones. I had experienced the sadness that naturally follows the passing of a grandparent or a great grandparent. These experiences were a part of life and not too difficult to cope with for my teenage or twenty-something self. I didn't expect the older generations of my family to live forever, and so while the news was upsetting, the feelings of sadness and loss passed in time.

My mother's parents were first. My grandfather died when I was very young, and I barely remember him. My grandmother passed when I was in high school. My grandmother's passing was somewhat sudden (heart attack), but not wholly unexpected, as her health had been poor for some time. It was then that I learned that our extended family only really saw each other at weddings and funerals. At the funeral home, my mother introduced me to her cousin Ruthie. Ruthie asked me if I knew her son, who went to my school. I started to respond that I didn't, when it suddenly clicked with me that he was that quiet guy who sat two seats behind me in religion class the previous year. I'd spent an entire year in class with my second cousin without even knowing who he was. Clearly at this time in my life, I didn't experience strong family ties.

In college, I had a deeper experience to grapple with. I remember that I was taking a mid-term exam when my father appeared at the classroom door. He motioned to me to come to the door. I tried to motion back that I couldn't, but he just motioned more vehemently that I needed to come NOW. My only thought was, "Who died?" I never asked it aloud. I was too afraid of the answer. I placed my test on the instructor's desk and exited the classroom. My father motioned for me to follow him and didn't say a word. We left the building in silence and got into the car with my mother waiting behind the wheel. When my parents traveled together, my mother was always the passenger; she never drove. Something was really wrong if my father wasn't driving.

As we pulled out of the parking lot, my mother let me know that my grandmother (my dad's mom) had died. My natural question, "What happened?"

was initially met with silence. Eventually my mother replied, "Self-inflicted gunshot wound." If I thought I was stunned before, I was wrong. I didn't know what to say, and just sat in silence until we reached my grandparents' house where my grandfather, my uncle and aunt, and my brothers and sister had gathered. We will never know for sure whether her death was an accident or intentional, but for me, my last interaction with her suddenly took on new meaning.

The last time I had spoken to my grandmother, she had come to see me perform as part of an a cappella singing group. After the show, we all left the theater together. It had been snowing, and the walkways were a little slick. As we were approaching the street where the cars were parked, my grandmother said, "I guess you're wondering why an old woman is walking so slow." I had never heard my grandmother talk like that in her life. She was eternally optimistic and always full of joy as long as I had known her. Not understanding what she meant, and a little confused, I replied, "No, not at all." Looking back, I could see that something had changed for her. Her self image had shifted drastically if she could refer to herself as "an old woman." I was told later that she had been suffering with depression for quite some time. I just wasn't around to see it. I was busy with my academic life in college.

I was fortunate to realize that I didn't know enough to recognize the signs of depression, and there wasn't anything to be gained from thinking that I should have, or could have, done something. But from that time on, I could now say that I did have experience with a loved one going through depression leading to suicide. From that time on, I took any mention of suicide or thinking about ending one's life very seriously. More than once I've been the one to reach out for professional help on behalf of a friend who was in trouble. I could recognize the signs now.

The time after my grandmother's passing was a very rough time for my family. It was right around Easter, and it put a damper on the holiday for years to come. Because it was so unexpected, it took a long time for those collective wounds to heal. And for as long as the sadness lingered for me, I can't even imagine what it must have been like for my father to lose his mother in that way.

At that time, I didn't have much experience with the grieving process. I didn't have anyone close to me to talk to who wasn't also experiencing and having to deal with their own feelings. And I had to keep up with my school work. I let the passage of time do the healing, rather than addressing how I was feeling directly. At that time I also didn't have a lot of experience working with deep emotions. Most of my life was lived at the mental level, in academia. It wasn't until I was in my 30s when I earned a Master's Degree in Spiritual Psychology that I would delve into the unplumbed depths of my own psyche.

A few years after my grandmother's passing, when I was in my mid-twenties, I got the call that my grandfather was in the hospital. He had been crossing the street near his house and had been struck by a car. Oddly enough, I DID know what that was like. When I was nine years old, I was struck by a car walking home from school. I remember waking up in the ambulance and asking my mother, "What happened?" She replied rather calmly, "You got hit by a car." I was fortunate that the station wagon wasn't going very fast on our neighborhood streets. And nine-year-olds mend relatively easily. I currently have only a scar under my chin to show for my ordeal. (Thirty stitches... which in one fell swoop put me ahead of my brother for total lifetime stitch count.) My nearly eighty-year-old grandfather would not be as fortunate. With both legs broken, he would have had a long, arduous recovery had he not died within two days of the accident.

I was at my grandfather's bedside when he passed, along with my aunt and uncle. Most of the rest of the family had gone home. They had been there all day, and I had arrived more recently. That was my first and only experience of being with someone as they took their last breath. One moment he was breathing, albeit laboredly. Then he took one final exhale, and his eyes opened slightly as his body fully relaxed for the last time. We shouted, "We love you, Grandpa!" as though his spirit would surely hear us as it finally freed itself from its mortal body.

While my grandfather's passing was sudden, we consoled ourselves saying that eighty years was a long life. He was now with his wife and could be happy.

These were my experiences with loss and grief in my growing-up years. As painful as the losses were, death has a certain finality about it that allows the passage of time to ultimately lift the sadness, especially for the younger me who saw the passing of an older generation as part of the natural way of things. But these experiences did not prepare me for what lay ahead, when my grief would become deeply personal. While the ideas and methods I present in this book assist many in healing through grief from the loss of a loved one, it was not death that taught me about grief. It was the break-up of my first relationship, which I will discuss in detail in Chapter 6: Why am I Crying?.

Exercise: Writing about your experience.

Write about your own experiences with grief. Journaling can provide a way to focus your thoughts and gain some perspective. You've chosen to read this book for a reason. Allow yourself to get in touch with what brought you to this place and time.

Notes

Notes

Chapter 3

Unresolved Grief

When we speak of grief, it is often associated with the death of a loved one. It is how we describe the emotions that show up after a loss of someone or something that is important to us. In truth, those emotions can show up after the loss of a job, a relationship, one's health, or just about anything. We associate "grief" with "loss."

For the purposes of this work, I am going to focus on *grieving* as a process. When we experience a loss, we enter a state of bereavement. It is the emotional sadness, loneliness, etc. which follow a loss that we label "grief." When we are ready (and not a moment sooner), we begin the process of grieving. In Western society, this is considered a natural process that goes on for an unspecified amount of time, often a year or so, and then we complete and "move on."

I am going to suggest that this model is inadequate. If you ask most people about the process, you will find that it is deeply personal, and everyone's story is different. But if you ask someone to describe in detail exactly how they moved from grieving to not grieving, they likely can't give you a point in time when they stopped grieving. For some people, years after a loss, they may not yet be done. Emotions can come in waves with varying expressions over long periods of time. And when you think you're done, you may find that there are more layers to be revealed, deeper depths to be plumbed. For others, they may be able to tell you they have come out the other side, into a state of acceptance.

In the remainder of this chapter I will focus on some of the books and teachings that provided me with key insights and understandings about the nature of grief and depression, and about how to heal my own depression through grieving.

The model of the grieving process that I was most familiar with growing up is the one put forward by Dr. Elisabeth Kübler-Ross: The five stages theory, from her 1969 book *On Death And Dying.*[1] The stages she wrote about were for people who were faced with their own imminent mortality. Later, the five stages; denial, anger, bargaining, depression,

---

1   Elisabeth Kübler-Ross, M.D., *On Death and Dying*, (New York, Scribner, 1969)

acceptance; came to be associated with the grieving process generally. In the theory, not everyone goes through all stages, nor do they go through them in order.

At this point I wish to note that the term "stages" tends to confuse people, as it implies that there is an order. From what I have seen, everyone's experience is unique to them. My encouragement to anyone is to make your own experience OK.

Later in the book, I will have more to say about this. For now, I will focus on two of the stages, depression and acceptance, and how they relate to the grieving process.

In book three of the series *Conversations with God*[2], Neale Donald Walsch writes about the five natural emotions. You can look up the excerpt of his discussion on the Internet[3]. He mentions that Elisabeth Kübler-Ross taught him about the five natural emotions, one of which is grief. He goes on to write that "grief that is continually repressed becomes chronic depression..." It is this relationship between depression and grief that I find most illuminating. Said another way, depression is unresolved grief.

---

2   Neale Donald Walsch, *Conversations with God*, (Charlottesville, Hampton Roads Publishing Company, Inc., 1998)
3   http://spiritlibrary.com/neale-donald-walsch/five-natural-emotions

I was reading an excerpt online[4] from the book *Lost Connections: Uncovering the Real Causes of Depression - and the Unexpected Solutions*[5] by Johann Hari. Hari writes about the clinical description of depression in the DSM (Diagnostic and Statistical Manual). The manual lays out the symptoms for recognizing depression. He relates how there is an "exception" when someone has experienced a loss, as otherwise every grieving person would be diagnosed with depression. Said another way, depression is unresolved grief.

When the DSM-V replaced the DSM-IV, the bereavement exclusion was, somewhat controversially, removed. My understanding is that it was considered more important to be able to diagnose major depression regardless of whether an individual is experiencing bereavement-related grief, as the consequences of not diagnosing major depression because of the exception outweighed the benefit of keeping the exception. I must stress that diagnosis of major depression must be from a competent, licensed professional. If you feel you need professional assistance, please seek it.

At this point, you may be asking, "Great, Mike, now what? So you're saying that my ever-present

4   https://www.theguardian.com/society/2018/jan/07/is-everything-you-think-you-know-about-depression-wrong-johann-hari-lost-connections
5   Johan Hari, *Lost Connections: Uncovering the Real Causes of Depression - and the Unexpected Solutions* (Bloomsbury USA, 2018)

malaise and bouts of deep depression may be related to my grief? How does this help?" And that is a fair question.

Before addressing how I and others have used the grieving process to find freedom from depression, I do want to state that not all depression is related to unresolved grief. I am not claiming I have "the one and only cure for depression." I highly recommend that anyone experiencing long-term depression seek professional assistance. If the underlying cause of depression is medical in nature, then by all means use an appropriate intervention. However, for someone who may be suffering from a prolonged grieving process, possibly with symptoms of depression, the ideas that follow in succeeding chapters may act as keys for working to bring the process to its natural completion... a state of acceptance. Acceptance allows the depression to lift.

As we continue on our journey together, I will relate my personal experience and the keys that I have found to be effective for me. These are the same stories I relate in my workshops and coaching to effectively assist others in the process of healing through the grieving process. My first truly deep experience of grief and depression stemmed from the break-up of my first relationship. But before I tell you about my experience, I will establish some basic premises about how emotions operate in human consciousness.

Chapter 4

A Model of Consciousness

In this chapter I lay out the model of human consciousness that the rest of the book uses. I have found that when workshop participants understand how emotions operate, they are able to better understand and use the grieving process to move into acceptance, healing, and empowerment.

If you understand the human consciousness model that I describe here, but don't buy into it, I invite you to suspend your argument with it temporarily. As an experiment, you can work with the concepts in this book and see if they work for you. If they do, consider a deeper look into the model. And when I say, "see if they work for you," what I mean is to ask yourself, "Do the concepts and ideas match my real-world experience?" Ultimately, that is the test of any model, theory, outline, etc.

And now... I present a basic model of consciousness.

For the purpose of explaining the grieving process, I will talk explicitly about three of the levels of human consciousness: physical, mental, and emotional. While my life centers around the spiritual level, I don't delve into that explicitly in this book. This may seem odd, as the grieving process can be a deeply spiritual one and can even awaken people to deeper levels inside themselves. While that is true, and I certainly relate to people in my workshops from that place, I have found a "spiritual view" of life is not required for the process of grieving and healing emotional pain to work.

I will now briefly describe the three levels of consciousness in a simplified way that we can use as the basis of our examination of the grieving process. For a more in-depth discussion of levels of consciousness, I invite you to read a beautiful book on the subject: *Loyalty to Your Soul: The Heart of Spiritual Psychology* by Drs. Ron and Mary Hulnick.[6]

The Physical Level

The first level of consciousness that we can readily observe is the physical level. This level is the level of our physical body and everything that goes

---

6   Mary R. Hulnick, Ph.D. and H. Ronald Hulnick, Ph.D., "Consciousness in a Nutshell," in *Loyalty to Your Soul* (Hay House, Inc., 2011). pp 53-89.

with that. It includes not only our physical body, its senses, and its various systems, but also our behaviors. It is everything about us that can be observed from outside of ourselves, and the mechanisms by which we observe others. To make the distinction: while the emotion of sadness is something we can experience internally, crying is a physical behavior that can be observed by someone else. Similarly, a thought or idea cannot be directly observed by another, but what we say or write about it can be. The physical level is directly observable.

The Mental Level

The next level of consciousness that we can grasp relatively easily is the mental level, or the mind. This includes all of our cognitive functions, like knowing, thinking, believing, reasoning, justifying, etc. The mind can act as a container, and as a processing engine. It holds our belief systems and our thoughts. It processes information, accesses memory, and draws conclusions based on what is already stored and what comes in from our physical senses.

The Emotional Level

The emotional level, for some people, can be a bit more mysterious. It is often the least well understood of the ego levels. (When I refer to the "ego," I'm referring to the mental and emotional levels and the will – the drive to make things happen.) I will spend a little extra time here, so I can be clear about how emotional responses occur. I will also draw a distinction between emotions and feelings. The terms are often used interchangeably, but I tend to think of *emotions* as originating from within our own consciousness (following from our beliefs and thought patterns) and *feelings* as what we sense from the outside. This will make sense to you if you are empathic (you can feel other people's emotions in your body).

Emotion Follows Thought

The ego levels of thought and emotion may appear independent, but they are very much related to one another. When someone experiences an emotional reaction, if they are then asked what the emotion was a response to, they will name an external event. "I got angry because my girlfriend ..." or "I was upset because the rain ruined our day outdoors." People tend to link the physical with the emotional, joined by the word "because." However, this is not the complete picture. If it were, then everyone would react the same way to the same external event, and that just isn't so.

For example, two people may have very different emotional reactions to "It's raining." A child on a baseball field may be devastated by the news. A farmer in a cornfield may be ecstatic. It's the same physical event, but two very different reactions.

Why? The child wants to be playing baseball, and he can't do that while it's raining. The farmer needs rain for her crops to grow.

It is their belief about what rain means to them that determines the emotional reaction they experience when the physical event "rain" occurs. If the child has a belief "It shouldn't rain when I want to play baseball," that may be followed by, "and it's just awful if it rains today." If the farmer has a belief, "My livelihood depends on adequate rain," that may be followed by, "and the rain today is much needed. I love it!"

Another way of saying this is, "Emotion follows thought." In everyday life, our emotional reactions to what we see and hear, and even smell or taste, can happen so quickly following the physical sensation that it's easy to conclude that the physical sensation *is the cause*. But I can tell you from experience that if I am willing to do the work to change my beliefs, I can change my emotional reactions. I will not claim that this is easy. It requires understanding and practice. For more information from a psychological perspective, read the article on Albert Ellis' Rational Emotive Behavior Therapy in Wikipedia[7]. There are a number of excellent references in the article footnotes as well.

---

7 https://en.wikipedia.org/wiki/Rational_emotive_behavior_therapy

One Roman philosopher stated it this way:

> "People are not disturbed by things, but by the view they take of them." - Epictetus

Right now, you don't need to know how to change your beliefs or thought process so that your emotional reactions will change. You only need to be open to the idea that when humans change their thinking about a situation, the emotions will naturally change. This is a key component to understanding how grieving can lead to acceptance and ultimately to healing emotional pain.

In the next chapter, I relate a story which illustrates how our perceptions and beliefs can shape how we feel about an event.

Chapter 5

Expectations

When I was 18, a co-worker of mine called me and asked me to come in and cover his shift one Sunday afternoon. He didn't initially tell me why he needed me to cover his shift, so when I showed up and he was dressed in a dark suit and tie, I naturally asked about it.

ME: "You're overdressed for answering the phones. What's going on?" I inquired.

ROB: "I have to go to a funeral for my uncle. He passed a few days ago."

ME: "I'm sorry to hear that. Is there anything I can do, besides covering your shift?"

ROB: "No. I'm fine. I appreciate you taking my shift for me so I can go to be with my family."

ME: "You don't seem that upset."

ROB: "We were expecting it. He was murdered."

I'm grateful that my sense of shock was bigger than the disconnect that was going on in my brain. My mind was searching for an explanation. Was he in the Mafia? the CIA? It made no sense. Once the initial shock wore off, it was all I could do not to laugh, with all the crazy notions that my mind was entertaining, attempting to understand something so implausible.

ME: "I'm going to pretend I know you well enough to ask how you could possibly have expected someone to be murdered. I know it's a stressful time, but did you hear how that sounds?"

ROB: "Oh, yeah, I guess that doesn't make sense." Rob almost started to laugh at himself. "He was mugged a couple of weeks ago and has been in a coma since then. The doctors said he wouldn't make it. We didn't know exactly how long, but we knew it was coming."

So, in essence, the shock of losing his uncle had come a couple weeks prior, with time to process and say good-bye while his uncle was still alive. The death itself was just the logical conclusion based on what had already occurred. My friend had already worked through the anger and the grief to a large degree. Of course there would likely be more tears as the family gathered one more time, but it would likely be a very different scene than if his uncle had been killed on the day he was mugged, with no time to say good-bye or deal with the emotional impact before having to acknowledge the reality of the situation.

Our beliefs and expectations shape our emotions. An unexpected death is shocking and can register in consciousness as a tremendous loss. An expected death may register as a completion.

Chapter 6

Why am I Crying?

What is the secret to working through feelings of sadness and loss? When it feels like this feeling will never go away, how do I cope?

When I was in my late 20s, I went through my first break up. Prior to that time, I'd never had a serious relationship. I had experienced the loss of older family members who had died, as I wrote about in an earlier chapter, but this was a different experience of grief. It was a relationship of two and a half years, and we had "broken up" a few times before, but this break up was different. The other break ups were the "I'm mad at you" kind—the kind that don't last. This one was the final break up. It was finally over. I knew it in my heart, and I was devastated.

I spent days just lying in bed and crying or weeping. When I thought I had no more tears left, another wave of emotion would show up. I thought my life as I knew it was over. My mind was churning on memories of some of the best times of my life, and some of the lower moments. Part of me wanted to be able to salvage the pieces of my broken heart, to find something to hold onto, but there was nothing.

At the time, I was in a class, obtaining my Master's Degree in Spiritual Psychology, where I happened to be working on my relationship with my father. Up until that point in my life, we hadn't been very close. Almost all of my phone conversations with my father lasted less than 5 minutes. He's not a phone talker. He'll talk your ear off in person, but not on the phone. And since I had moved across the country just three years prior, with the telephone as the only mode of communication (before Skype existed), our relationship hadn't improved since I'd left. But because I was engaged in a process of observing the relationship and taking small steps to improve it, I called my dad. The conversation went something like this:

ME: "Hi, Dad."

DAD: "Hi, Mike. So... did you want to try and install that computer thing? What's it called?"

ME: "Um, no. That's not why I called."

DAD: "Ok. Well. What do you want?"

ME: "Eric and I just broke up."

DAD: "Oh. (pause) You just want me to listen."

ME: "Yeah."

At this point, I'm thinking, *"Who are you, and what have you done with my father?"*

We talked for three hours. And he *listened*. He shared with me about his first girlfriend and how that break up felt. We talked and talked...and talked. And that was the first time in my life I'd had a heart-to-heart talk with my dad. I asked him about it... why we never had. He said, "Well, you never needed it. You were the good kid. The other three had some serious challenges in their lives, but you never really did."

I didn't feel so alone in my sorrow any more. I was still sad, still crying, still depressed... but I wasn't alone.

The next day, as I was shuffling from the kitchen to the bedroom, an odd thought entered my mind.

"Why am I crying over a relationship I <u>say</u> I don't want?"

The water works stopped instantly. The cloud lifted. And suddenly I could see what was going on. I was crying over what I thought it <u>could</u> have been. In my mind, I kept thinking, *"If only he this"* and *"If only we that."* If only... if only... if only. I was crying over my fantasy relationship. The relationship I had wasn't working. After two and a half years, it was pretty clear... he wasn't going to change into the person I wished he would be. He could only be who he was. Nor could I become what he wanted. I could only be who I was. Expecting anything different was simply setting myself up for heartbreak, which is exactly what I was experiencing.

Now what?

Now I could set about the business of grieving. "What do you mean?" you might ask. "Hadn't you been grieving for the last three days?" No... not really. I'd been crying and depressed. I'd been feeling sad and lonely. I hadn't done any grieving. The dictionary will tell you that "grief" is deep sorrow, especially when caused by someone's death. And it will tell you that "to grieve" is to suffer grief, to mourn.

I will suggest that we modify the definition of grieving somewhat to better understand how to move from sadness and depression into acceptance and healing.

The process of grieving is the process of letting go of the *fantasy* relationship.

We *feel grief* when we experience a loss. Our picture of reality—how we think the world should be—doesn't match physical world reality—how it is.

In my mind, I had created my ideal relationship with my boyfriend. Sure it didn't match up sometimes... maybe most of the time. But that didn't stop me from nurturing the fantasy, giving it a life of its own. In my world, he was the perfect boyfriend. When the disparity between my *image* of him and *who he was* became too great, a break up was inevitable. And when the break up occurred, I was suddenly left with a very large gap in my consciousness between the way that I thought my life was going and the way it actually was. My idea of my future included my boyfriend in it. I created that future over the previous two and a half years. As long as I held onto that fantasy future, I would feel the loss. It didn't match my current life.

In my moment of clarity, I began to dismantle that unreal future. That was the first step on my journey to healing my heart and coming back into balance emotionally.

Let me be clear... the man I broke up with actually *is* a great guy, and we are still friends. While we were in relationship, I didn't understand that I was creating an unrealistic image with expectations that no one could live up to.

In the next chapter, we'll look at how perceptions and expectations can influence the grieving process.

Chapter 7

Grace's Story

Once I was in a hotel lobby talking with a woman, I'll call her Grace, whose father had recently passed from a brain tumor. That kind of tumor is one of the worst. I knew from my own experience. A friend of mine was diagnosed and passed within four months. It can be very difficult on a family.

I was sharing with Grace about the grieving process and how the *perception of loss* is shaped by our picture of the future (a desire for a fantasy future). A woman sitting nearby overheard what I was saying and immediately got upset. "That just isn't so!" she exclaimed. "Grief is a natural emotion everyone experiences after a death, and there is no avoiding it. If there are no tears or anger (outward signs of grieving), then you are trying to bypass the process and it will just be bottled up and cause emotional problems later."

After the woman left the conversation. Grace said, "You know, I really didn't have any of that going on when my father passed. It felt like a burden had lifted, and I felt at peace. I wondered if I was bypassing my emotions at the time, but now, after listening to you, I realize that I had done my grieving over the last few months *before* he died. I was very glad for the time I was able to spend with my father. We really got to talk about a lot of things and clear up some miscommunications between us. I felt very clear in our relationship at the end."

Grace had let go of her fantasy future where her father was alive for the next ten or twenty years. She grieved the perceived loss *before her father passed* and moved into acceptance of the current situation as it was presenting itself to her. She was able to use the time she had to connect with her father and heal their relationship while he was alive.

Grace's story also highlights a common misconception that grieving the loss of a loved one must be dramatic to show just how much you loved the person. "If I'm not crying my eyes out, that means I didn't really love them," is a common sentiment. I'm going to suggest a radical notion. You ARE love. That is your nature. The love that you have for someone, that you experience when you're with someone, is inside you—it *is* you. It's still there when someone you love dies. You get to keep it.

Your emotional reaction to the perceived loss is independent of the love that you have for the person. **The degree of inner emotional disturbance (whether or not expressed outwardly) is an indicator of the degree of *attachment to your ideas* of what the future was supposed to look like.** My friend Grace had already come to terms with her father's impending passing from the physical world. When the event occurred, it was in alignment with her world view at that time. Her expectations were matched by physical world reality. Thus she didn't experience sorrow and loss at the time of her father's death.

This isn't to say that she didn't experience sorrow and a sense of loss. It simply had occurred earlier. She had had months to adjust to the new reality that her father would not be in her life much longer. She had experienced the usual feelings of shock, loss, and grief; and she had worked through all of that and come into alignment with the shape her relationship with her father was now taking. She was able to use the time that she had while her father was alive to complete that relationship, rather than staying in denial, only to have to grieve her father's passing after he died.

Chapter 8

Un-happy Anniversary

The writer W. S. Merwin reflected, "Every year without knowing it I have passed the day..." referring to the anniversary of his death.

I've heard of people who use the day six months opposite their birthday to acknowledge their death day. You may have heard the phrase to "use death as your ally." It's a way of using the anticipation of our own death to realign our inner compass. Understanding and contemplating that we are here for a finite amount of time can be a powerful way of awakening to a more depthful sense of purpose and meaning in our lives.

Such a reminder that we are only alive for a finite amount of time can assist us with using our time on this earth well. It is a reminder to truly live before we die.

When a loved one dies, their day of passing creates an anniversary. The anniversary of the death of someone we were close to can bring sadness and grief with it. I have known friends who have become dysfunctional on such an anniversary, especially in the first year or two after an event. My grandmother died very close to Easter, and for years afterward my family had some sadness around Easter Sunday, whether or not it coincided with the actual date of my grandmother's passing. It was a powerful association.

What does it mean when the sadness comes up and feels the same as it did a year ago? It means there is another opportunity to grieve. This is OK and natural. Remember that the feelings of loss and sadness arise because of the distance between physical world reality and the way we think things *should be*. If I haven't fully grieved the fantasy image of how life *should be* different than the way that it is, the anniversary of the original event can bring up those same feelings.

If I use the time just after a death to grieve... If I use the wake and the funeral, sitting shiva, or any other ritual to bring my consciousness into alignment with the new reality where my friend or family member is not here physically, then the anniversary doesn't need to be a sad time. It can be a joyous time of remembering. But if I have not yet been willing to release my ideas about how life should be that are incompatible with the way things are, I set up a rift in my consciousness which results in feelings of separation, loss, sadness, etc. I may be able to forget temporarily by distracting myself, but unresolved feelings have a way of resurfacing.

The good news is that any sad feelings are indicators of where the work is to be done. Feelings follow thought. As the feelings come up, I can take the opportunity to observe my thought process and become aware of the beliefs or mental images I'm holding on to which may be the source of the sadness and ongoing sense of loss.

Exercise: Language as a key.

Do you have an anniversary related to unresolved grief? If yes, take time to write about your beliefs about the situation. Are there ideas you are still holding onto that are in conflict with the reality of the situation? What language do you use when you think or speak about the event. For example, "When (s)he was taken from me..." is an example that points to a belief that the person should still be here. Look at the language you use to uncover your underlying beliefs.

Is there an opportunity to update your language, the way you communicate about the situation, that is more in alignment with the way things are, rather than how you would like them to be? For example, "When his/her life was completed..." acknowledges that I cannot say that the person should be alive, and I accept their passing with equanimity. The next chapter illustrates this principle.

Notes

Notes

Chapter 9

Complete or Incomplete?

Do you consider your loved one's life complete? ... or incomplete?

Grief, feeling deep sadness, is a natural response to the loss of a loved one. Whether we consider their life as whole and complete or as incomplete has an enormous impact on how we feel. In my workshops, I will often ask the question, "Do you consider your loved one's life complete?... or incomplete?" Most people can readily answer the question. If the person passed peacefully at the end of a long life, the answer might be, "It was complete." If the loved one died younger, or if the person I'm working with just isn't ready to accept their passing, they will answer, "Incomplete." I then follow up with, "How do you know? What are you using as a reference point?" The response is a window into their world. They are telling me their ideas about how they think their loved one's life *should* have been.

But how can *anyone* know for sure that someone else's life is incomplete? I may have many reasons to call someone's life incomplete, but unless I know their life's purpose and why they embodied in the first place, for me to say that their life is incomplete is presumptuous. I may have some beliefs about how long people *should* live, or what it means to have fulfilled one's life purpose, but ultimately, at the time of death, every life is complete. It is complete in the sense that there is nothing left. When I accept that, regardless of the person's age, health, or other circumstances, the healing process can begin.

If I refuse to accept that a person's life is complete when they die, then I can get stuck in a form of denial and keep my fantasy future alive inside myself. Holding that duality in consciousness, that they should have lived longer and that I know what should have happened, while simultaneously knowing that they are no longer alive, maintains and feeds the feelings of deep sadness and loss.

In the next chapter, I relate a story that illustrates one way to make the shift from "incomplete" to "complete."

Chapter 10

Clearing Misunderstandings

In one of my early workshops, I was working with a dear friend of mine from Iraq. Raad (his real name, pronounced similar to Rod, but you have to roll the R a bit) had recently lost his mother. He was having a difficult time because his 86-year-old mother had died after a friend had given her some chocolate that she wasn't supposed to have. The friend didn't know Raad's mom shouldn't have chocolate. His mom knew, but perhaps didn't fully understand the potential consequences. Late one night, she had decided to eat the chocolate and then had trouble breathing. She was taken to the hospital. When Raad arrived at the hospital, he was informed that his mother had already passed. He was instantly stricken with grief. He collapsed on the floor sobbing, devastated.

"She could easily have lived to 90!" Raad exclaimed in the workshop, when I asked if his mother's life was complete or incomplete.

Holding that thought to be true could mean four years of feeling the sadness and loss. As long as he held onto the belief that his mother should still be alive, there would be a rift in his consciousness. He was setting himself up to experience another four years of grief. In modern psychological terms, Raad was in partial denial about how death can come unannounced. After four years, Raad would be living in a world where his mother could have died of other causes, and so the process of grieving could truly begin. To hold the two incompatible stories —"my mother should still be alive" and "my mother is dead"—is a declaration of the unwillingness to grieve.

During the course of our interaction, Raad related to me a story from his childhood. He had been in the shower when the boiler caught on fire. His mother came to rescue him, but was unable to reach him initially. She went into a such full panic that she could no longer stand. Yet she persisted, crawling on all fours. She would not give up, and eventually was able to find Raad and pull him out of the house. Raad told me the story with tears streaming down his face.

I asked him if he were to have told the story a year ago, would he be feeling the same way? He replied that when he told the story in the past, it was a powerful image of loving. It was something that he carried to remind him of his mother's great love for him. He felt that true unconditional love from a mother very deeply. But in the present moment, he told the story with great anguish. I asked him what had changed. He spoke almost inaudibly, "I couldn't save her."

I held Raad's gaze, looked into his eyes, and held him in my heart. I said simply, "That wasn't your job. You didn't need to save your 86-year-old mother from dying. That wasn't your job." I paused for a moment, then continued, "It may have been her job as a mother to save your life all those years ago, but it was never your job to save your mother from death."

Raad looked at me for a moment, and then suddenly burst out laughing. Inside himself, in that moment, he accepted that keeping his mother alive was not his responsibility. His mother had known that her doctors had told her not to have chocolate, and she chose to eat it anyway, when no one else was around. We will never know for sure if his mother was fully aware of the potential consequences, but Raad was able to give her the dignity of making her own choices.

For the previous two years, Raad had been on a mission to save his mother's life, and all the while her health had been continually deteriorating. Through accepting events as they happened, **without attempting to insist that his mother live longer**, or that the circumstances of her passing should have been different, he was able to release the judgment (misperception) that he was somehow responsible for preventing his mother's death. Raad was able to shift his memory of his mother saving his life back to a powerful image of loving.

Now I will introduce a core concept in this work: *the gap.*

Chapter 11

Mind the Gap (The gap is in your mind.)

In this chapter I will use some simple diagrams to illustrate how we relate to reality. Consider that we relate to our past as memory, and to our future as a projected fantasy. The projected future is often based on past experience, but can also be pure fantasy. The present is our current reality as we experience it now.

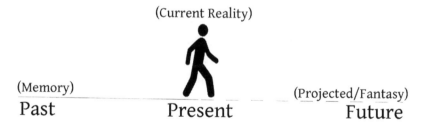

(Current Reality)

(Memory)   (Projected/Fantasy)

Past   Present   Future

When I experience a loss, what does that mean? Something that was there isn't there any more. More precisely, something that was in my projected future isn't in my current reality. I will illustrate this by showing the divergence between physical world reality and what was my projected fantasy future at the time the loss occurred.

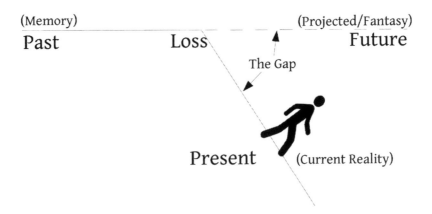

In the above figure, you can see that when a loss occurs, reality diverges from the future as I saw it at the point of loss. This is completely natural. Everyone carries around an image of what tomorrow will look like. When I experience loss, it is because reality has changed and does not match my idea of what my future was supposed to be. I now have what I call a *gap* in my consciousness.

Recall that toward the end of chapter 6, where I relate my break up with my first boyfriend, I briefly mentioned how I had created a gap in my consciousness. If you go back and review that chapter, you will see how it illustrates the concept of *the gap*. Notice how I enter into the sadness and depression when I realize that my world has changed, my relationship is over, and I'm wishing for the future where I still have the relationship. I feel the impact of the *loss* of relationship.

When I realized what I was doing – holding onto a fantasy future that simply didn't match reality, only then could I set about the work of letting go of that future and closing the gap in my mind. Once I could see it, then the emotions became my ally. I could use my sadness to point me in the direction of what I needed to see, accept, and complete inside myself. And in time the sadness faded, as I aligned myself with my new future, and new opportunities.

In the next chapter, I'll relate a story that illustrates the concept of the gap in the context of losing a job.

Chapter 12

Joe's Story

In one of my workshops, a bright man in his forties with wavy hair was complaining about how he had lost his job. I'll call him Joe. Joe worked for the U.S. Government, and honestly thought he couldn't be fired. It's notoriously difficult to lose a government job. He had had what he thought was a minor misunderstanding with his boss, but apparently his boss hadn't thought it was minor. His boss had gone back to his job application from twenty years prior, uncovered a not insignificant error, and had him terminated from his position. This man told me that he had been a good worker, carrying more than his share of the load. He felt like he had been "stabbed in the back." Joe had seen a vindictive streak in his boss at times, but nothing like this.

And now there were days, Joe related to the group, that he just couldn't get out of bed. He felt his world was collapsing around him. This was a sign that Joe was headed for (or already in a state of) depression.

In the workshop, we talked about the concept of "the gap," and how he was taking his twenty years of working at that job and projecting it into his future. His belief that he couldn't be fired was so strong that he wasn't relating to his current situation as someone who was looking for a new job, but rather as someone who was a victim of the system, who had a job that he wasn't allowed to work at.

Joe was in serious denial. As I was suddenly thinking of Stephen Root's portrayal of Milton Waddams (the guy with the red Swinger stapler) in the 1999 film *Office Space*, I wondered just how wide the gap in Joe's consciousness was, and what it would take to bridge that gap.

Joe and the group continued the conversation, delving deeper into Joe's job situation. Joe related that over the past couple of years, his job had become more challenging—not his work, but the job. While in the past he and his co-workers had mostly gotten along, the current political climate had shaken things up a bit. His office was not one that was normally affected by political changes in the administration, but most recent election cycle had had a polarizing effect in other offices that were connected, and the energy of it was spilling over into Joe's workplace. Before he was terminated, there were days that he dreaded going into the office.

I saw an opportunity for Joe to examine more deeply what was going on with his relationship to his job, his co-workers, and management. I asked Joe if he was really unhappy at his job? Yes, he was, but he thought eventually things would settle down. This was a slightly more subtle form of denial. He was holding what seemed like a false hope that things would be different in the future. There wasn't really any indication that the workplace climate would improve anytime soon. This sort of "false hope" scenario creates a positive future fantasy that cannot be fulfilled. Does this sound familiar? It should. Given the framework we're exploring, it can be seen as another type of gap. As long as Joe was holding onto the idea that his workplace environment "should" be as it had been before, in contrast to the actual environment, he would have a gap in consciousness, resulting in his feeling averse to going into the office some days.

I could see that, in a sense, Joe's situation had a similarity to my situation after my first break up. In my case, my moment of realization came in the form of, "Why am I crying over a relationship I say I don't want?" In Joe's case, why was he complaining about losing a job where he was unhappy? The opportunity that naturally presented itself was to grieve the fantasy that the job could ever be what it had been before the recent political shifts. It was clear to me, but I didn't know if Joe was ready to see it, or to accept the possibility that everything that had unfolded was *for* him, not *against* him.

As we continued our work in the group, looking at the reality of the situation vs Joe's ideal that was a projection from his past, he gradually began to see how he was creating his current feelings through his thought process. In his mind, he was constantly re-living the last few weeks and all of the turmoil that went with it. He was also holding onto the idea that he still wanted his job, based on his memories from years ago. I reminded him of the story I had told the group earlier about my break up and my realization. I asked if he saw the similarity. He did. I asked how it might help him in his current situation.

"Well," he hesitated, "If I look at my job as the significant other that I just broke up with, I can see how I'm crying over something that doesn't look like it was working. I also see how it's a little different in that I'm telling myself that I do still want my job, but you're right... I want the job I had, not the job it had become. I guess it really is similar."

Joe indicated that he wanted to sit with this concept for a while, and as it was time for the lunch break, we concluded there. When Joe left the workshop that evening, he had a clear direction for the work he needed to do. I didn't have an opportunity to follow up with him, so I don't know for sure if he was able to find resolution within himself. I definitely consider Joe's story an instructive one for understanding the process of loss and grieving, and I wish him well.

Now that I've shown you what *the gap* is through these illustrations, let's take a look at how it relates to grieving. In the next chapter, we will take a deeper look at specific responses to the gap in consciousness that is created when we perceive a loss.

Chapter 13

Going Deeper

How we approach loss shapes the grieving process. At the University of Santa Monica, they say "How you relate to the issue is the issue." This is very true in the realm of grief and loss. How we respond to the perception of "loss" will determine our experience as we work through the feelings that surface in these types of situations.

In Chapter 3, I mentioned the five "stages" of the grieving process as outlined by Dr. Elisabeth Kübler-Ross. Now that we have a new framework for looking at how the perception of "loss" occurs in consciousness, let's take a look at how each of these stages operate. Recall the five stages: denial, anger, bargaining, depression, acceptance.

Before we look at each of these individually, I feel it is important to repeat that the term "stages" is considered a misnomer these days. Dr. Kübler-Ross was working with individuals diagnosed with terminal illness. She saw patterns that she labeled as stages for her theory. In my experience, the grieving process doesn't appear in "stages." Someone who has suffered a loss may express any, all, or none of these common experiences and in any order. There is no real pattern or progression. What is important is to work with the feelings that are present. Allow yourself to have your own experience, and allow others the dignity of their own experiences.

I have found in my workshops that it is helpful to look at these five common experiences relative to our framework, as many people are familiar with them. We will take a look at each one individually.

Denial

What does denial mean? What am I denying? I am denying reality. I'm saying to myself, "It just isn't so!" I am simultaneously saying that I know what is so–that nothing has changed. I am clinging to my fantasy future as if it were reality. I am walking the path of my projected future and ignoring physical world reality.

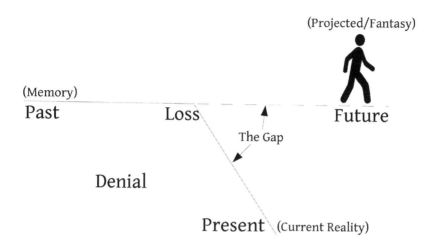

(Projected/Fantasy)

(Memory)

Past   Loss   ▲   Future

The Gap

Denial

Present (Current Reality)

The longer I walk the path of denial, the wider the gap becomes, and the harder it will hit when I am forced to reckon with the physical world having changed, even if I don't want it do.

Anger

What is anger? According to the Buddha, "Holding on to anger is like grasping a hot coal with the intent of throwing it at someone else; you are the one who gets burned." It is a fiery emotion, and normally directed at someone or something. But how does it relate to the gap?

Oddly enough, in this model it's not really related. Why not? It's important to understand what drives anger. In my experience, anger is most often a "cover up." There is always something underneath. A depthful discussion of anger is beyond the scope of this book, but I will give a sketch of how it operates and what fuels it, so you can understand why it can show up alongside grief.

I've participated in workshops where the participants were encouraged to express their anger in a healthy way. We weren't allowed to direct it at what we perceived was the source (parents, spouses, teachers, ex's, etc.), even in the imagination (no psychic violence). It was expressed with the voice or with body movement, in a way where no one would be injured. Invariably, when the anger was allowed to be fully expressed, not just a temporary catharsis, underneath was hurt. Most people would break down at some point into tears.

If those tears were encouraged, and the hurt and emotional pain were allowed to be fully expressed, another layer would emerge: caring. We don't feel hurt over things we don't care about. We don't get angry over things we don't care about. Something has gone awry with something we care about deeply.

And what is underneath the caring? Love. We care about that which we love. Thus the fundamental energy that fuels anger is love, albeit through a misperception.

So why does anger often show up when someone is in the grieving process? If I lose a quarter, I don't really enter into the deep sadness of grief. If I lose something I care deeply about, that's when I can feel pain, hurt, and sadness, and we call it grief because there is a loss. Some people go straight to expressing their grief through tears. Some people aren't ready to be in the pain of feeling the loss, so they may respond with anger.

In this sense, whether a person responds to a loss with anger or tears has to do with their underlying beliefs about the situation. Yet it isn't really related to our framework of the process of grieving, how we deal with the gap in consciousness.

Bargaining

What is bargaining? This response is very much related to the gap that occurs with a perceived loss. We've either come out of denial, or skipped over denial. **We are willing to see the situation as it is. But, we don't want it to be that way.** While not living in the projected future, the bargaining response is basically saying, "I'm not yet willing to let go of my idea of how the world should be, and I'll go to great lengths to restore the world to the way it was."

In the image that follows, you can see the bargainer attempting to change reality to match his idea of how things "should" be, in order to close the gap. Ultimately, this approach is futile, perpetuating the feelings of sadness and symptoms of depression. And yet it is my experience that many people go through this a few times before realizing the futility of it.

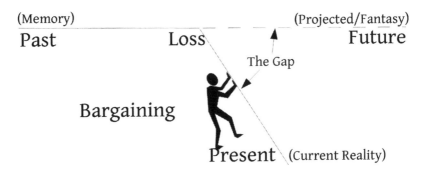

Understand that to some degree, this approach makes sense to the mind. If it were possible to alter reality, that would close the gap in consciousness, which is what you ultimately want. Consider a scenario where I thought I lost a relationship (dumped via text), and then soon after found out that the text was meant for someone else. Balance is restored, the gap is closed... because my idea of reality has come back into alignment with my fantasy future. The perceived loss was the illusion in this case, and I only experienced sadness and grief briefly. However, this is rare. Most often we have to deal with the loss and find another way to close the gap to restore balance.

Depression

I've stated more than once that "depression is unresolved grief." (It is important to note that depression may have other causes. If you are experiencing depression, I recommend that you seek professional assistance. It's OK to reach out and get help.) In the context of the grieving process, the symptoms of depression can show up quickly when a loss occurs. In fact those symptoms are the natural response to a perception of loss of something we care about. Most people understand this, which is why there had been an *exception* for the time following a loss where we don't attempt to treat the symptoms of depression with medication or other interventions. If an individual naturally grieves the loss (closes the gap and accepts the new future without the loved one/job/success/relationship), balance is restored. But if the individual holds onto the projected fantasy future, maintaining the gap, the symptoms of depression may continue indefinitely, ultimately resulting in a diagnosis of depression. The "depression" was there all along, but after a time the exception goes away. What does this look like?

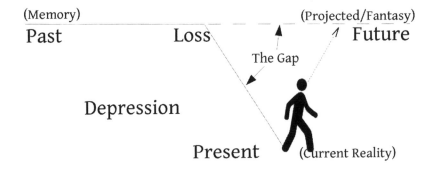

It looks like not fully accepting things as they are. Notice the person in the figure living in the current reality, but still focused on the old fantasy future. The situation "should" be different. They "shouldn't" have died so young. I "shouldn't" have been fired. The word "should" is a key to identifying a judgment present. It's a misperception that divides consciousness. There's the way it *is*, and the way it *should* be. And the individual above doesn't like the way it is. It's that division that maintains *the gap*, and if left ungrieved, all the symptoms of depression may continue.

Acceptance

When we do the grief work, we close the gap. We release the judgments we have about the situation. We're no longer wishing for something different, or demanding that the world be different than the way that it is. And it's not just a lip-service acceptance: *saying* I'm aligned with reality, but in my heart still clinging to a fantasy reality. Through the process of forgiving any judgments (using "forgive" like to forgive a loan), we dissolve the judgments, release the misperceptions, and come into alignment that everything has unfolded as intended. We make peace with the old projected future, and let it go. When the acceptance truly takes hold, there is often a sigh of relief. It is done, and we just know it. The gap is closed. A new future is created.

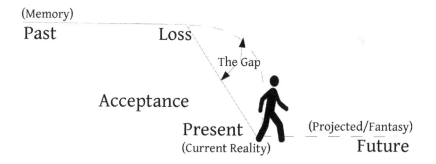

It is important to know that this process may not be an easy one. When I work with individuals on grieving related to a loved one, I will ask about their religious beliefs, spiritual experiences, etc. How an individual closes the gap is most often, in my experience, dependent on how they see their life, the life of the other person (in the case of death), and their relationship in that context. Ultimately the gap is closed based on life experience, which is deeply personal. There is no "one size fits all" solution. I do believe that everyone can find a way to close the gap. It takes time.

Exercise: Becoming more aware of the gap.

I've covered the main misconceptions people have around grief, and I've used some stories as examples to illustrate the process by which you can become more aware of the gap. There is a saying based in Gestalt therapy that simple awareness is often curative. The process of healing though grief begins with an awareness of the gap between physical world reality and the imagined future.

1. Identify the perceived loss. What was there that is no longer there - Examples: a person (death, distance, etc.), a job/career, a relationship, etc.
2. Identify the two futures
   a) What is my fantasy or projected future, where the person is still alive, or I still have the job/career/relationship, etc?
   b) What does the future look like based on physical world reality, where the person/job/career/relationship, etc. is not present?
3. How am I relating to these two futures? Write about your feelings.
4. Am I holding onto the fantasy future? In other words, am I holding onto the idea that the person *should not* have died, I *should* still have

"my" job, I *should* still be in the relationship, etc?

5. Am I willing to let go of the fantasy future? Am I willing to cry every tear, and allow my consciousness to align with present reality?

Please understand, this is not a "five steps and you're done" type of process. The grieving process takes time, and everyone is on their own timeline. What this process does is to help clarify *what* you are grieving. You are not grieving what was lost. **You are grieving your *idea* of how things should have been.** Understanding that can give you tremendous leverage in doing the actual grieving work, and lifting out of the feelings of sadness and depression, or whatever best describes your emotions as you deal with the sense of loss.

Remember that emotions follow thought. "Doing the emotional work" means using your emotions as a guide to let you know where the work in consciousness needs to be done. You feel a sense of loss because something that existed for you no longer exists. That is natural and normal. The change in the physical world sets up the gap in consciousness, again quite natural. And the way to bring yourself back into balance is through re-aligning with the way things are in physical world reality. As you release the projected future, you bring yourself back into balance mentally and emotionally.

Notes

Notes

Chapter 14

Empowerment

The purpose of this work is to empower people to use the grieving process to heal the gap in consciousness that gives rise to the symptoms of depression. But what does it mean to empower someone? What kind of power are we talking about?

The power of this work lies in your choices. Through an understanding of the mental and emotional aspects of grief, you have choices that you may not have been aware of before. The good news is that you have new options for working through grief and coming back into balance. You have a greater awareness of grieving and how it affects your life. You also have a greater responsibility for your life and your future. You can take the opportunity to do the grief work and heal, but it is not required or guaranteed simply because you have awareness.

Some years after my mother passed, I was visiting my father. I could tell he was still struggling. This was about the time that I was just beginning to develop *Healing through Grief* as a workshop, and I took the opportunity to sit with my father and have a deeper discussion about what he was going through. I asked him if he would be open to learning about the process of grieving, and how he could use it to make a shift in his life. He agreed and we had a long discussion.

At some point, I got the sense that he was getting that "eyes glazed over" look. He was still nodding his head, but not really engaged in the conversation. I took some time to pause and check my perception about what he had absorbed.

ME: "How are you doing with all of this? Are you following me so far?"

DAD: "Yes."

ME: "So you understand that the sadness that you're feeling now is based on your idea that Mom should still be alive?"

DAD: "Yes."

ME: "Do you think you can find a way to see her life as complete? Can you trust that God knew what He was doing when He called her home?"

(silence)

ME: "You still wish she were alive, don't you?"

(pause)

DAD: "Yes. I just can't let her go. I feel like it would be disloyal to her memory."

ME: "I really hear you, Dad. And you get to keep the memories, and the love. It seems like you're taking those memories and attempting to put them into your future. You can honor her memory and the life you shared and still let go of the idea that she should still be with you in this part of your life."

DAD: "I just can't. I don't know how."

Tears followed. My dad wasn't ready to let go. After 43 years of marriage and a few years of living alone, his desire to live in the future he had imagined for himself where he and my mother lived much longer was stronger than the desire to let go of the sadness. I think in some ways he had become used to the sadness, like an old blanket. It wasn't really serving him, but he was unwilling to give it up.

A few years after this conversation, my father began showing signs of, and was eventually diagnosed with, a form of dementia. He is no longer able to speak in sentences, and he has difficulty understanding what is said to him. I sometimes think about whether I could have assisted him further when we could still talk about these things. And yet I know I must honor his path in life and his choices.

Understanding what is underneath the feelings of sadness and grief does not of itself change the feelings. It gives you some leverage in that you know where the work is to be done, when you are ready. And even when you are ready to make the choice to see the gap and close the gap, it still takes time. This work does not take away the pain. As I wrote earlier, you have to cry every tear. This work can help to shorten the time you spend in the sadness, when you become clear about what it is that you are letting go.

Chapter 15

Transformation

I want to emphasize that grief is not something to be avoided. While the information in this book is presented to assist you in working through feelings of loss and coming back into balance, it is important to understand that the process of grieving is often transformational. For every individual the experience of loss, feelings of depression, process of grieving, and eventual surrender into acceptance is a very personal journey. Learning *about* something will bring you knowledge. Having the *experience* will lead to wisdom.

I encourage people to journal about their experiences throughout the journey from loss to acceptance and freedom. The opportunities for self-reflection, self-compassion, and self-revelation are many when we are faced with the gap in consciousness that comes from loss. There is an old saying that what doesn't kill you makes you stronger, and I believe there is some truth to that. As painful as the process is, it is also an opportunity to find an inner strength that may have been untapped.

For myself, I can say that my experiences of grieving showed me that I was capable of surviving much more than I had previously thought I could. And with every experience that took me deeper into the emotions of sadness, despair, and depression and then back out again into the Light, I found that my capacity to hold for others increased. I knew pain, and it wasn't just my pain. When I can see pain in someone's eyes, there is a knowing in me, empathy opens my heart, and I can be with someone in their suffering. That is the essence of compassion. (The prefix "com" means "with," and "passion" means "suffering," as in "The Passion of the Christ." So to "have compassion" for someone is to "suffer with" them.)

As you go through the grieving process, with a greater understanding of what you are grieving, be open to what the process has to teach you about yourself and about your capacity to be in relationship with others compassionately and in a soulful way.

Chapter 16

Transcendence

U ntil now, I have focused on the mental and emotional levels of consciousness as they relate to the process of grieving. I would be remiss if I did not include a chapter focused on the spiritual opportunities present when we find ourselves grieving, especially the loss of a loved one.

The pain that often follows the sudden loss of relationship when someone dies can be not only transformative, but also a gateway. In the midst of the sadness and grief, we can become aware of that part of ourselves that is ever-present, observing from a place of neutrality, as we delve into the depths of sorrow. We can become aware of our higher nature, supporting and loving us through all that we are experiencing. And if we have the wit to truly, deeply surrender to the Loving that is the essence of who we are, we can become aware that we are aware.

I find myself at a loss for words. We haven't really invented a common language to describe experiences which transcend the mind and emotions. If you've had such an experience that I am ill-equipped to describe, no words are needed. You know. And if you have not yet had such an experience, no words can convey the experience, any more than my attempting to *describe* eating a watermelon could possibly be anything close to the experience. And yet I feel that it can be useful to point in the direction of what is available through those experiences which tend to break down the ego. The ego is limited in its comprehension. Thus one of the best ways to move beyond the ego is to experience the incomprehensible.

All this to say that when the time comes, allow yourself to be cradled in the arms of Spirit (or God... however you choose to put words on the experience). Use the experience of loss and the process of grieving as a springboard to come out of the emotional depths and find your True Self. Ultimately, healing through grief can be cleansing, purifying, freeing, and uplifting, if you choose to follow the upward path. You may know you have come through to the other side of your grief when you find yourself inexplicably in the presence of Joy. Everyone's journey is unique to them.

Chapter 17

Summary

H ere I will summarize the key concepts of *Healing through Grief: Finding Freedom from Depression.* You can use this chapter as a refresher if you find yourself needing to be reminded of what you have learned through these pages. You may also wish to write some notes for yourself to personalize and integrate your learnings.

This book is entitled *Healing through Grief: Finding Freedom from Depression* because grieving is the healing agent that releases us from the cycle of depression. Recall that when we experience a perceived loss, it creates a gap in consciousness. That gap is the precursor to the feeling we call grief. The symptoms are the same as the symptoms for depression, and so it may be more accurate to say that the gap is a precursor to what we call depression.

The process of grieving is the process of closing the gap. The gap is the difference between our perception of reality and an alternate or fantasy reality we want to keep alive. This alternate reality is something we create naturally, as we have the capacity to consider our future. It matches our present reality until something happens that makes present reality diverge.

It's also possible to create a fantasy future from nothing and attach to that. For example, if I meet someone and imagine a relationship with the person, perhaps without ever even speaking to them, I've created a gap. If I nurture this fantasy relationship, I can find myself in a state of depression, pining for a relationship that never existed in physical world reality. The mechanism that creates the feelings of depression is the same.

Additionally, it's possible to create a fantasy past. For example, if I had a rough childhood, and later in life I create the fantasy childhood the way I wished mine would have been, and then attach to that, I've created a gap. I can find myself in a state of depression when I think about my past. While some would suggest that I grieve my childhood, it is the fantasy childhood that I must grieve and let go of. There may be other work to be done to heal childhood wounds, but that is beyond the scope of this book.

Through simply being aware that *what* we are grieving is the fantasy future, or alternative future, that doesn't match physical-world reality, we do the work in consciousness to close the gap and come into a state of acceptance. Assuming we will do this sooner or later, understanding the process assists us in doing it sooner. If we choose to attach to the alternate or fantasy future, we can become caught in a cycle of depression.

Denial and bargaining can be natural temporary responses to a loss. They can also lead us into depression of we hold onto those responses too long.

Anger is born from our loving and caring, filtered through judgment. We release the anger by releasing the judgment that underlies it. It's not necessarily related to the grieving process.

When we close the gap, we come into acceptance. Our projected future changes to match physical-world reality more closely. Along the way, there may be opportunities for transformation, coming to new understandings about ourselves and the world. There may also be opportunities for transcendent experiences, surrendering to the Divine within ourselves. Everyone's journey is unique.

I will leave you with this reminder: emotions are not something to be fixed. They are windows to the soul. You don't need to "do" anything with emotions. They will shift on their own. They simply need to be acknowledged and expressed. The best thing you can do for someone who is in the grieving process is to listen, without judgment or commentary, as they express what they are going through.

May you have grace on your life's journey. You have my love and support.

Notes

Notes

About the Author

Michael Polek is an author, workshop facilitator, and technical administrator living in Los Angeles, California. He has been an avid student of personal growth and development for over twenty years. Michael earned his Bachelor's Degree in Computer Science and Mathematics from Loyola University Maryland (then Loyola College in Maryland) in 1990. He earned Master's Degrees from the University of Maryland in Computer Science in 1995 and from the University of Santa Monica in Spiritual Psychology in 2000. He also received Certificates in Consciousness, Health, and Healing and Soul-Centered Leadership from the University of Santa Monica in 2002 and 2005, respectively. Michael is also a graduate of Insight Seminars, including *Insight IV: Knowing the Purpose of Your Heart*, a professional seminar.

Michael is an active minister in the Church of the Movement of Spiritual Inner Awareness. His ministry is one of service in the community through volunteering and working with individuals and groups to bring about healing and transformation. He has facilitated workshops in Southern California and the Midwest.

Michael enjoys playing beach volleyball on the weekends and traveling to experience different cultures. His favorite countries so far are Argentina, Egypt, and Israel.

56084320R00061

Made in the USA
Columbia, SC
20 April 2019